MACHINES AT WORK

Under the Ground

Henry Pluckrose

FRANKLIN WATTS

NEW YORK • LONDON • SYDNEY

Most of the time
we live above ground.
But sometimes
people go below ground.

Perhaps they work in the
basement of a tall building.

To get below ground
they might use stairs
or an escalator.

Basements are often used
to store things safely.

Beneath many banks
strong rooms keep
valuable things safe.

Some people go below ground
to catch an underground train.

Underground trains move people quickly from one place to another.

The control room for the underground railway is full of machines.

They control the trains, the signals and the destination boards.

Underground trains
travel through tunnels.

Sometimes cars
go through tunnels, too.

Tunnels can be cut
through land or under the sea.

Machines are used to dig tunnels.
First a shaft (a large hole)
is dug in the ground.

Then the machines
that dig the tunnel
are lowered down this shaft.

A tunnel boring machine
cuts (or bores) through the earth.

The tunnel walls are strengthened with iron, steel and concrete.

A lot happens beneath the street.
There are tracks and pipes,
cables and drains.

Machines are used
to dig tunnels for these,
and to lay the pipes and cables.

Machines are also used
to carry out repairs under ground.

Even further beneath our feet,
deep inside the earth,
there are many different
layers of rocks.

Some layers contain metals.
Others contain coal.
Rocks can be mined
by machines under the ground.

Coal is mined
by a cutter
that breaks the
coal into pieces.

The pieces are
loaded on to
a moving belt.

There are layers of rock
beneath the sea, too.
Sometimes they contain oil.

To reach the oil
a hole is drilled
from an oil rig.

oil rig

sea

rock

drill

oil

Glossary

basement the part of a building below ground

coal is mined from the ground and is burnt to make heat and electricity

basement

escalator a moving staircase

mining getting valuable materials from rocks in the ground

oil rig a structure from which people drill for oil

shaft a hole in the ground leading to a mine or tunnel

strong room a room with thick walls that protects valuable things

tunnel a passage under the ground

Index

bank 9
basement 6, 9

cable 20
car 14
coal 23, 24
control room 12
cutter 24

destination board 13

escalator 7

oil 26, 27

oil rig

pipe 20

rock 22, 23

sea 15, 26, 27

train 13
tunnel 14, 15, 16, 17, 18, 19
tunnel boring machine 18

underground railway 12
underground train 10, 11

tunnel